OUR FIRST CANOEING VACATION

By

Joseph Stanaland

CONTENTS

TIPPIE-CANOE

I've wanted a canoe ever since I can remember. Consequently, most of my friends think I'm crazy; they'd much rather crank up an outboard and roar off down the lake in a shower of water skiers. Personally though, I always like the water and woods because they were more peaceful and quiet than the city where I grew up. Fortunately, I married a girl who agrees. At 107 lbs. she's the most determined paddler, the most intrepid explorer, and the most cheerful dog-goned camper you ever saw.

Of course, I'll admit even she was a little startled last Spring when I pulled out a well-thumbed brochure and first suggested that we spend all our vacation money (and then some) on the canoe, its accessories, and nearly 50 other items of assorted camp gear, clothing, and supplies we didn't already have. But she bounced back quickly, and before you could say "monthly installments" we were commissioning the "Tippie-Canoe" in the distant waters of Lake Hiwassee, North Carolina.

That five-day shake-down cruise was a real eye-opener. Boy, what I'd forgotten about camping out! And, boy, did it rain! It _poured_ for five solid days, and we'd planned on cooking over open fires. Needless to say, we didn't; and I don't think our clothes are quite dry yet. But, even so, we learned the things we needed to know for the _real_ adventure later in the summer --- an eight-day, camping out, 115-mile paddle through the most beautiful mountain country in the Southeast. This time, we went prepared for the worst and found the best in weather, thrills, and contentment.

Like most modern-day canoeists, we carried our boat to the starting-point on a car-top rack. Our duffle was housed in four rubberized bags, old military surplus we'd bought at the local "Army" Store, and occupied the trunk of the car, along with the paddles and boat cushions, until we laid it amidships in the "Tippie-Canoe".

And that's <u>all</u> it took… a good boat, four bags of assorted gear, a healthy wife, and a driver.

THE DRIVE TO "LOST BRIDGE"

The "Driver" is the guy you had brass enough to approach about driving you 175 miles into the heart of the mountains and then bringing your car back home. He's usually the fellow, too, who'd meet you later at some pre-arranged spot, unless there was a second friend who'd share the chore. On this trip, our originating driver was an old friend, more the Daytona Beach type, but willing, at least, to humor our eccentricities. Besides, it was a refreshing drive for all concerned northeast from Atlanta, through the "Blue Ridge", "Snowbird" and "Cowee" ranges, into Nantahala National Forest, among the southern toes of the "Great Smokey Mountains".

Anyone appreciates a ride like that, though probably not as much as Shirley and I. Our enthusiasm had been at fever pitch for weeks, through days of noon-hour shopping and through nights of studying maps and making plans. And, here we were at last, winding up the little mountain highway past Murphy, North Carolina, toward the apex of a great gorge in the region the Cherokees called "Nantahala" (the land of the noonday sun).

We passed through Topton, N.C. about one o'clock and stopped at a small roadside restaurant for lunch. Fortunately, it was a fine one, the kind with which you like to start a long trek into uncertainty. But the proprietor, when told of our plans, joined the long list of those who thought we'd lost our minds! He asserted with frightening finality that anyone canoeing down the Nantahala River at power lever would never be heard from again, and that anyone trying to go down any other time would need wheels. We, at least, proved him right on the latter point.

Nantahala Dam, above us, wasn't making power that day, and the cold clear water of the stream was fighting a losing battle against the "noonday sun". What there was left trickled around the rocks paving the stream-course.

Luckily, however, there was an alternate route in our plans, and we drove on down the Gorge to investigate it. At the foot, where Nantahala empties into giant Fontana Reservoir, we angled away eastward, up, over and down the ridge and across the finger of lake that beckons the "Little Tennessee River" into the same lazy repose. Now at Lauada, we cut sharply back paralleling this new stream at a distance. But our highway now was cut high into the mountainside. Glimpses of the river were poor and infrequent. From the distance, it too looked rocky, but then, so does the Atlantic Coastal Shelf from a half mile up! There was no surer test until finally, we sidled down to the shore at a crossing alarmingly called "Lost Bridge".

The water was a little swift, and the steppingstones less steady than they appeared, so Walt, our driver, got his neat slacks wet to the knees. Still, it was quite a lark... until we watched the car re-cross "Lost Bridge" and disappear toward home. What a strange, lonely feeling for two "tenderfeet"!

You know that, now, you're strictly on your own. Before you, there's 10 or 12 miles of river you know nothing about, 3 lakes totaling around 47 miles, 3 massive dams (and a fourth under construction), and then over 56 more miles of river. But you can't turn back now, and besides, up ahead, there lies the adventure of things you've never done before, in places you've never seen before.

INTO THE GREAT UNKNOWN

We pushed off into the current at 2:30 p.m. on a cloudy-bright Sunday afternoon. The water was not so hurried as it looked at first but, still, moving right along. Shoals of rock were with us from the beginning, angling across the entire width of the stream, but there were broken places, and we learned to recognize them through the changes in the water's turbulence. Of course, at this point, most everything had <u>some</u> water over it, and poor aim meant only a momentary jolt and a little lost paint.

Meanwhile, I, personally, was loafing along, devoting lots of time to the fancy camera we'd borrowed and giving little thought to anything past the next bend. I should have noticed the rocks in my camera sights were getting bigger and bigger and bigger! As a matter of fact, the water was beginning to look lost among them. And we started scraping worse and worse. Finally, we ground to a complete stop.

My 160 lbs. plus Shirley's 107 and the duffle's maybe 150 is no great load for a 17-foot aluminum canoe with air tanks, but you couldn't have sailed a child's toy over some of those shoals. So, we went over the side, to enter the element in which we would spend most of the next 9 or 10 miles. The footing, at least, was good. A carpet-like, brown moss that overgrew the rocky bottom, and we whooped at the exhilaration of sudden contact with the cold mountain water.

From then on, it was in-the-boat-out-again, push, pull, carry, drag, choose a channel, try another. By evening, we were exhausted. The still-flat remains of an old farm road on the shore became our first campsite. I cleared the ground and pitched the tent; Shirley prepared supper, a pattern we followed from then on.

Our tent was a 6x8 foot "pup", with sewn-in floor and a zip-in mosquito net front. The walls were "balloon-cloth" and gave us a big weight advantage in traveling. It was easy to erect and surprisingly steady considering that it was pegged with wooden stakes in rocky ground. I'll sure buy or make myself some <u>steel</u> tent stakes next time I travel in the mountains!

Shirley did all our cooking over a two-burner, propane gas stove. It was a real dandy that folded into a neat, square box with a carrying handle. Of course, we stowed it, like everything else, in one of the waterproof bags when we were underway.

But the tent and the stove were just two of the major pieces of equipment. From the other 93 items on the checklist, I can't think of a single one we failed to need at one time or another.

ENJOY THE BITTER WITH
THE SWEET AND THE SPOIL
WITH THE SPILLS

I was up about 6:30 the next morning and had hot coffee for Shirley by the time she was dressed. We sat on a rock to drink it and watched the little river sliding swiftly past our bare feet. It had risen a few inches over its level of the previous afternoon... still no torrent... but our survey let to the conviction that we'd do more paddling and less wading than before. That just goes to show you how wrong you can be!

By the time we'd finished a good bacon and egg breakfast, washed the dishes, and struck the tent, the sun was well up. At least, we were better dressed for the occasion that day... no long trousers to sop up water when we had to go over the side, and no uncovered feet to get nicked and stone bruised. Instead, our personal duffle included just the right solution, shorts and stout canvas play-shoes with heavy rubber soles. Better attired, we were able to laugh off the disappointment of the water's continued shallowness and settled down to really enjoy the trip.

The stream was a fascinating challenge. Sometimes it idled along in pools 25 or 30 paddle-strokes long; then, suddenly, it would incline and go bucking and plunging and twisting down a block-long grade. You could play navigator and helmsman all you wanted, but, nine times out of ten, the route you chose was no better and no worse than any of the others. And the added velocity of the water over the shoals and around the great boulders sometimes changed your course quite unexpectedly.

Along the shore there was an endless variety of mountain forests and fields and pastures. Unpainted little farmhouses often revealed the inquisitive, but shy, faces of their children... white, red-cheeked little faces half-hid behind a tree, joined at last by a suddenly bold hand waving as we passed from view. We saw mountain folks in the water, too, all trout fishing, with the water swirling up about the knees of their faded overalls. They faced down-stream, usually, following the drift of their lines, and they seldom knew of our presence until we coasted (or splashed) up behind them.

Our greetings were always returned politely, but with that firmness and reserve that marks the southern mountain man... an all concealing mask that hides curiosity, anger, amusement, even the momentary shock of our sudden appearance.

Further downstream, however, we found a pair who weren't able to muster their dignity... for they were minus clothes. It was in one of those relatively quiet pools where we were able to paddle a little. Around the bend we came, and there they were, perhaps 30 yards away. At sight of Shirley, they doubled over and dashed for the cover of shore. We tried not to laugh, but who could have avoided it?

Lunchtime came, and we pulled over to a shady bank for sandwiches. It's surprising how quickly you can learn to like plain, ordinary water with no ice in it, and it's amazing, too, how much good a box of cookies will do. Riding the river in a canoe is like riding a horse; you've just got to relax and enjoy the bitter with the sweet, the spoil with the spills. I even invented a new paddling technique I decided to call "Gondola Style", in which you sit side-saddle on the stern and pole along until you have to slide off so as to lighten the load.

But we were glad to see Fontana Lake come at last. We'd been on the river 25 hours, including the night, and were dog-tired from a final, mile-long forest of giant boulders and low falls. Here, finally, was dark, still water and another man fishing, but, this time, from a boat with an outboard motor.

A narrow channel now bore us smoothly westward and under the very bridge over which our car had crossed to Lauada the day before. Drinking water was low, so we pulled in long enough to hike up the highway for supplies. This mission success-fully accomplished, we set out to find our second campsite.

Places to camp are hard to come by on man-made mountain lakes; we'd learned that before, on the trip to Hiwassee. The great dams just keep piling water back until the valleys and ravines are filled and only the mountaintops stick out. The slopes are so steep, in most places, that it's a good trick to <u>climb</u> up them, much less pitch a tent there. The best alternative is preceded by a right or left turn into a likely-looking cove. If you're lucky, you find that it's the mouth of a sizeable creek, whose course has come (like our river) down a more gently inclined piece of real estate. And there you will camp. If you're not lucky, and darkness catches you, you sleep in the boat. We were glad we never had to do so.

As a matter of fact, we found our creek mouth on the first try after entering Fontana. It was boarded by hard-packed earth, completely devoid of shrubs or weeds, and traces of previous fires testified that we were not the first ones there. Its only drawback was the 8-foot high, muddy band left by the Lake's seasonal withdrawal, but we dug steps with the trenching tool, and we were "home" for the night.

Our little expedition covered the next thirty miles in two days, punctuated by a step at another excellent campsite and a brief refuge from a storm.

The campsite was the unexpected kind, a flat-topped mountain spur that projected from the southern shore and gave us a magnificent view of the "smokies" in the north. Again, there was the charcoal of many fires to evidence the ceaseless popularity of a good place to sleep and eat.

GETTING INTO A RHYTHM

As usual, we had begin looking for a place to stop about six o'clock. Pitching camp in the dark is difficult and more than a little dangerous. It's hard to forsake the lake that time of day, though. The wind had died and left the surface ideally calm. A single stroke of the paddle sends your canoe coasting smoothly across thirty or forty yards of water. You quit talking and enjoy the silence. And, as the sun settles down for the night, your reveries are rarely disturbed by even the distant hum of a fisherman's motor or the flat smack of a leaping bass.

On a trip like ours, that's when you'd better look out! If you don't, you'll be trying to curl up in the boat for a long cool night, or you'll be playing "footsy" with a copperhead or a rattler as you stake your tent in the dark.

The early mornings are like the evenings... the water still sleeping, the fish breakfasting in noisy bounds... but there's something new added. It's the delicate mists which overspread the lake and tiptoe up the long, grooved mountain slopes. They're the famous trademark from which the "Smokies" take their name.

Once again, you'd love to get your boat gliding, but breakfast is a powerful inducement too, and there are the dishes to wash ands the tent to pack. So, you content yourself with a brief solo spin about the campsite while the food is on the fire and perhaps fish a little if you've the inclination.

The lake's surface isn't always so conducive to paddling, though. Mid-morning and mid-afternoon usually find a still breeze blowing across the great open stretches. Your back muscles begin to feel the strain of the added effort, and you chart your course to take advantage of every wind-breaking cliff or point of land that can be found. Even then, the fury of a high-velocity mountain storm is too much. On our second day with Fontana we met one and finally gave in before it.

The wind that afternoon had sprung upon us full-grown, and, unlike previous days, blew steadily and with a growing intensity. We foolishly clawed on against it, reluctant to lose time when we knew only three more miles would bring us to Fontana Village Boat Dock.

The waves slammed into us from dead ahead, and the bow soared up one and plunged into the next. We stopped paddling to put on our lifejackets and were swept back forty yards. Still, we fought on, confident that the white caps beginning to foam around us would shortly subside.

Ominous black clouds boiled out of a mountain kind's caldron to the west and swooped down toward the surface of the water. Now, event the temporary shelter of a large island was behind us. We were in the middle of a cast expanse of turbulent sea with a craft in which most of our friends back home had said they wouldn't even sit beside the dock. However, it's a tribute to that very boat that we came through safely. Its inherent buoyancy, plus the extra lift of the boats air tank, kept us dancing above the most dangerous troughs. We had only to fight the determination of the wind to swing the nose around. Had it succeeded in reaching our 17-foot broadside, I think we'd have rolled like a pencil.

But good steerage was only part of the fight, and our forward motion was obviously being rapidly reduced toward a complete standstill. Our arms were aching with weariness and our hands were raw and blistered. A fine rain was rocketing down the wind, stinging our faces like an undogged limb full of pine needles. There was nothing else to do but seek some form of shelter.

Gradually, we tacked toward the nearer coast and, finally, found refuge in the mouth of a large creek. We were wet to the skin, and, by the time we reached the shore and climbed out to "regroup" a little, the canoe was floorboard-deep in rain and spray.

That's one of the many times on the trip that I learned to know and appreciate even more the woman I'd married a brief year before. Tired as she was, with her hair stringing down her forehead and her wet clothes clinging limply, she walked ten paces, dropped to her knees and screamed with childish delight that she'd found a bear's tracks! And she had.

The old bruin had apparently come down for a drink the night before and then retired again to the solitude of the tangled underbrush above the beach. But he'd left his great four-footed signature, claw and all, sharply printed in the damp sand. I think Shirley would cheerfully have waited there the rest of the week to witness his return, but the storm passed shortly, and we were anxious to reach Fontana Boat Dock and inquire about routes for by-passing the Dam.

THE KINDNESS OF STRANGERS

I hadn't shaved since we left home, and my grizzled countenance definitely added something to our appearance as we approached the landing. This was no more fisherman's departure point either, but rather the waterfront facility of a well-known resort.

Clean people in crisp sport shirts and well-pressed Bermuda shorts stood about in groups awaiting the departure of the big launces that would take them out for a gentle box supper. We were regarded, I'm afraid, as something of an eyesore; and, closeup, the glamor of our quaint appearance (that had brought passing waves from these same hands in the days before) seemed to wave.

We had cold drinks and learned from the proprietor that the most gentle portage about the Dam was a three-mile trek! It was too late in the day to worry much about it then, however, so we took our departure and followed the retreating sun on down to the great structure itself.

Want a magnificent creating of man it is, stretched across the end of the lake for a city block or more, high as a three-story building above the surface and reared 400 feet above the river behind. We were truly awe struck at the sight of it. In fact, we hated so to lose the view that we camped directly across the channel and sat up late into the night watching the white crosses of light that shimmered along its rim and lamenting the fact that we had flashbulbs but no more film.

Next morning, we struck camp and paddled again directly to it. Above us it towered like the Parliament Buildings above Thames. At one end, an impassably steep bank rose to the highway, but, at the other, we found a steel pontoon dock provided by the Government, and a concrete stairway that climbed sharply through in immaculately trimmed park. Once at the top we saw the observation towers and information offices of the T.V.A. What a pleasure still to remember the kind people who helped us on our way! They began with the information officer on duty there, who, when asked for his suggestion of a quicker portage, temporarily closed his office to assist us.

A short drive in his car located a work-crew lunching in the small picnic area they were trimming. We told them of our plans and after a good-natured ribbing about out "vacation", which sounded to them, they said, like just a lot of hard work, secured agreement to meet us shortly with a pick-up truck. Our guide returned us to the head of the stairs and even helped me carry part of our duffle up the long climb. Shirley and I managed the canoe between us by taking it in easy stages.

Fontana Village is a lovely place situated on a great slope of the Cheoah Mountains. It's near the Appalachian Trail. There are modern stores and resort dwellings, even a theatre. But we had interest in civilization beyond the procurement of supplies and film. Our truck driver was an amicable fellow who undoubtedly would have stopped for this purpose had we asked him, but we hated to impose more than necessary, and allowed him to carry us through, instead, down to Lake Cheoah, which emerges from the turbines of Fontana Dam. Once there, we unloaded our gear and rode back up to the village where we bade him a grateful goodbye.

The groceries we bought there were heavy, and we faced an arduous walk back to the boat. What's more, we hadn't even paused to fill the water bag and canteens in passing through, and they were too empty to ignore. As we performed this task at the hydrant of a road-side service station, its owner inquired about our situation, and, once again, we discovered the willingness of people everywhere to help, that added so much to the pleasure and success of our trip. He and his wide-eyed little boy drove us back to Cheoah and the boat.

We found the water there so cold the canoe's metal skin had already become sweaty with condensation. No wonder! The waters of Lake Cheoah are drawn from Fontana Reservoir 400 feet beneath its surface! This made an excellent natural refrigerator. We took the fresh pork chops and eggs we'd purchased, wrapped them in foil, and laid them inside against the hull of the boat; and, I even decided to trail my canteen, for a time, tied to the stern rope. (These civilians just have to have their comforts.)

The new lake was one of the loveliest bodies of water we'd ever seen... clear as crystal... and it traced seven miles of mountain highway with a bank of lush growth. It wasn't wide, really more like a river than a lake, though there was no perceptible current. A few miles beyond our starting point it passed the power house to which water is piped from Santeetlah Dam, about five miles to the South. Here Cheoah was augmented in volume, but there was little change noticeable in the flow or width of the channel.

Toward evening, we exercised again our creek-hunting trick for a place to spend the night. It was more difficult here, for the road (though screened by trees) offered a high embankment on one side; and a sheer mountain slope composed the other. It grew later and later, and it looked as it our luck had run out. But, then, in the twilight, we made out and indentation in the mountainside, and within it, the projecting surface of a large, flat rock. Investigation proved it the entrance to another ideal site.

Human hands had terraced the slope with native rock in three places, and we chose the uppermost of these to pitch the tent. It was a soft glen, deep in fallen leaves, bordered in fern. The brook separated a few yards above it and one branch bubbled down each side of the area, the closer perhaps five yards away.

As I worked to erect the tent, Shirley arranged her stove and foodstuffs and, soon, the delightful aroma of frying pork chops seasoned the air about us. She added mixed vegetables and hot coffee to the menu, and we ambled down to the great rock beside the water to eat.

It was the only fresh meat we had during the trip, and sitting there, watching darkness close over the motionless surface of the lake, we experienced a double sense of satisfaction and well-being. We could see the lights of occasional cars on the highway across the water, but the sound scarcely reached us. And it was again one of those times when you just don't talk.

Shortly thereafter, we unzipped the front of the tent and undressed for the night. The little brook, mumbling to itself behind our heads, soon lulled us to sleep.

QUITE THE CONUNDRUM

We traversed the remainder of Cheoah in about three hours and arrived at its end shortly after noon. The lake narrowed here, of course, so that the highway on our right was separated from the Alcoa power house, on our left, by only the narrow width of Cheoah Dam. Since the road represented the natural portage route, we eased along that shore to within perhaps a dozen yards of the lofty concrete barricade itself and tied bow and stern to the few trees that grew along the bank. About 30 feet up, almost directly over our heads, stood the low retaining wall of a scenic overlook.

I climbed to it with difficulty and studied the situation. The highway continued on past the dam and cork-screwed sharply down the mountainside to a bridge in the deep distance below. From that point a dirt road doubled back along the edge of the lower lake toward the sheer back of the dam. Even from there, access to the new lake was complicated by a heavily over-grown, rocky slope, but that was the least of our worries at the moment. We had still to raise our boat and all its contents from Cheoah to the road level and negotiate the narrow, winding highway to the bridge.

My first thought was to do as we had in Fontana, seek help from the folks who maintained the Dam. But this was made difficult by a large, locked gate that barred passage to the power and administration buildings on the other side.

There were two alternatives. First, I could return to the boat, and we could paddle to the other side. But this meant heading directly toward the turbine intake, across the face of ten or twelve overflow gates, the latter of which, we presumed, could be opened at a moment's notice; and, thus far, no one except a few motorists had appeared to note our presence. An accident like that is probably unlikely but we, wisely or naively, never quit being apprehensive when we were within range of the possible suction.

Alternative Number Two meant a long walk down the mountain, across the bridge and all the way back up the other side. My mind, call it efficient or just lazy, calculated that if I were going to walk down the mountain anyway, I might just as well carry the canoe along. After all, we'd bought a carrying yoke for that very purpose. So, that settled it.

We carried our luggage up to the stone parapet, piece by piece. It was a treacherous pull in the midst of cascading small stones and inadequate handholds, and under a broiling sun, but at last the heavier items were all moved. A lazier, pitcher-catcher arrangement on the little ones brought our first loss. Shirley's canteen, unfortunately, contained just enough water to hover encouragingly on the surface for a moment before it plunged into the depths before the Dam.

Now, I moved the empty boat down to the very corner of the Dam itself. With a paddle, I handed the bowline up to Shirley, who had walked around. She held it firmly over the top guard-rail as I climbed the 20 feet up the rough wall to join her. Between us, we began to hoist, using the rail as a fulcrum. It was hard work! The canoe with its floorboards weighed over 80 pounds and I had to exert part of my strength to keep the rope far enough from the wall to prevent the bottom's scraping. What a job! It took us 20 minutes and a half-box of cookies to recover, but there "Tippie-Canoe" sat, looking strangely out of place beside the highway, and inviting me to make good of my plan to carry her to the next lake.

We decided that Shirley would help me get the yoke settled on my shoulder, then remain to watch over the rest of our gear. I'd leave the boat on the dirt road, far below, and return for another load.

Well, things started out that way. She helped me get started, as planned, and I wobbled off down the highway and around the first hairpin turn. The canoe, from the beginning, seemed out of balance (I learned later that I had the carrying yoke mounted backward), and I began immediately to feel the strain of holding the bow high enough to see where I was going. Until this moment, I'd never even practiced for such a portage, so I soon became aware of another problem. This was the yawing of the boat back and forth before the stiff wind which blew up from the valley below. I felt like the pivot pin under a giant compass needle.

To add to my woes, the highway had no real shoulder to it. What little there was between the edge of the concrete and the steel guard fence was badly over-grown. Consequently, I was forced to walk in the roadway itself, with the momentary expectation of being run down by the car which I imagined whipping around the sharp curve behind me or the blind curve in front. It was at this point that my right ankle twisted.

I'll never know whether it was the relentless swinging of the bow, a rough spot on the pavement, or my preoccupation with the fact that the leather pads of the carrying yoke were sliding off my sweaty shoulders, but the result was a spread-eagle sprawl right on the center-stripe. My outstretched arms had been trying to balance the boat, and the right gunnel now smashed my hand flat against the pavement. At the same time, the legs of my trousers grated away, and I slid to a stop on my bare knees and forearms.

The pain from the injured hand was blinding; I was sure it was broken. But, above everything else, there reoccurred the sudden fear of being run down by a car! This supplied a spurt of energy to even the apparently useless hand. I dragged myself from beneath the hull and desperately pulled it as close to the guard rail as possible. Scratched paint didn't concern me at the moment.

I just stood there for a few moments, leaning with the boat against the rail, and fighting the nausea which the pain from my hand produced. Then, I called Shirley, who was still within earshot around the curve. She responded immediately and brought with her those soothing and sympathetic words that wives use to repair damaged husbands. My hand began to feel somewhat better, and I decided perhaps it wasn't broken after all. So, despite Shirley's protests, I picked up the monster and resumed the downhill comedy, partly to ease my damaged male ego and partly because there wasn't any other choice, anyway.

This time I reached the bridge without further incident and deposited the canoe as far back up the dirt road as my waning strength would carry it. But hard luck was apparently through with us for the day. I had scarcely gotten back to Shirley when a carload of hospitable Florida tourists stopped to view the dam, saw our predicament and offered to ferry everything still left down to the bridge. One of the men even scampered down the embankment below the dirt road to help me lower our canoe into the water. We were in Calderwood Lake at last and with most of the afternoon still before us.

CALDERWOOD AND A KID

Calderwood has much in common with Lake Cheoah but possesses a unique quality as well. Like the latter, it's river-ish in appearance, narrow and long. But Calderwood has no highway, or road of any sort, along its boarders. It's completely isolated, and, during our passage, there was no other boat or human to be seen. The shores rise to sizable peaks and are covered with dense undergrowth. This is particularly true of the Southern ban, which, for several miles, is a national game preserve. The water here, also, was icy cold. Occasionally I trailed my injured hand in it to alleviate the sullen pain and prevent swelling.

Each bend we rounded produced a fresh view of idyllic scenery... lovely tree-clad mountains as far as the eye could see, the nearest ones, reflecting, with the clouds, in the water. Our course was west, now north, now south as we followed the deep channel's sweep from one canyon to another, but, strangely, the wind seemed always behind us. It ricocheted, we supposed, from one passage to another like the water. Even so, we tired as the evening advanced, and the tailwind appeared to be doing a lot less helping than it had halting when we were back on Fontana. The truth of the matter was that the labors and wounds of the portage were overcoming us.

Muscles down the small of my back felt like they were tied in knots, and no amount of position-changing seemed to avail. Shirley, I knew, was feeling the same, for she suddenly took a deep interest in our whereabouts and in how far it was to the next dam.

This was a somewhat difficult question to answer. The beautiful, big TVA navigation maps that we had used in Fontana were of no assistance once we entered the Alcoa lakes, and I had, for reference, only a topographical map prepared by the U.S. Geological Survey. As nearly as I could calculate, though, we were, at that time, about one big bend from the end of the line. It seemed like hours to our tired bodies before we made it, but, sure enough, as we made the turn, the lonely, lovely Calderwood Dam stood before us, some several hundred yards distant. We had traversed about fifteen current-less miles that day in addition to the ill-fated and time-consuming portage from Lake Cheoah.

Calderwood Dam stands between two great, rocky cliffs. As you approach, the one on the left appears almost vertical. The right bank is also steep but has been cut for a dirt road, which climbs sharply to the paved highway about a mile away. This dam's construction is quite unusual in that the back (or river) side falls straight down to a large circular basin, which, in turn, over-flows to reform the Little Tennessee River. The sheer drop is per-haps 200 feet, still faced to the left and right by the solid canyon walls. Direct human passage to the stream below is by parachute, a helicopter, or a torturous steel stairway that must be entered through the dam's usually locked superstructure. What bothered us just as much as we stood looking over the great overflow gates was the barren rockiness of the river below. Was this to be the ter-minus of the trip? Certainly no one seemed available to help us.

We had drawn up to the small floating catwalk about 6:00 p.m. and climbed the ladder to the top, but no one was to be seen. The only sounds of life emanated from a tiny white kit (the goat variety) who baaa'd plaintively from the side of the cliff. He seemed to be imprisoned high on a ledge whose surface crumbled into tiny landslides at every faltering step he took.

But we could give him no aid. The bare face of the wall was more than a match for an unequipped climber, particularly an amateur. Even had I reached him, the return, several hundred feet downward carrying him in my arms, would have been impos-sible. So, with a sense of sadness, we turned our thoughts toward finding the caretaker of what must be our home for the night.

No amount of shouting or searching could avail, however. The doors were locked, and our voices only echoed hollowly along the rails of the derrick track and against the sealed doors of the power house.

The thought of sleep on the Dam was a lonely one and even

a little frightening, for, in the deceptive twilight, it seemed to have a personality of its own. The moans of automatic turbines seeped up through the concrete from the vaults below, and the water gurgled and swirled hungrily as it was dragged through the power flume. We settled, instead, on the side of the dirt access road where it splayed out to enter a locked gate at the end of the Dam, and hoped that a sudden midnight cloudburst wouldn't send water cascading down the mountain-long gulley and carry is and the tent down the iron-barred drain before our door.

Shirley prepared supper in the light from clock-set spotlights which illuminated the scene as day disappeared behind the mountain at our backs. We sat for a time listening to the poor orphan on the canyon wall and wondered if he would fall prey during the night to a bear, a panther, or to his own insecure footing. Then, we turned in to a better night's sleep than we expected.

I was only too happy the next morning to put aside a half-eaten breakfast while I talked with three men who had just arrived by pick-up truck. They were Alcoa maintenance men planning to sandblast and paint the steelwork of the Dam before us. From them we learned that the river was easily navigable after a short distance; and, with that same generosity that we had encountered in everyone we met, they offered us passage to the highway and around the mountain by truck. Still more men arrived as Shirley and I finished packing, and, with ample help, the canoe was lifted vertically from its over-night mooring to the level of the road.

As we started to depart, we mentioned our little friend on the cliff, but the track driver laughingly pointed him out, now following eight or ten adult goats along a ledge even more precarious than that of the night before.

Without difficulty, we proceeded to Calderwood Ferry and embarked for the many river miles which would carry us to our final destination. The workman, having courteously refused our every attempt to pay him for the drive, turned to his truck and drove off in the crisp morning air, while Shirley and I, elated at having gotten around what we considered to be our last major obstacle, introduced "Tippie-Canoe" to a swift current.

WHAT A SIGHT IT MUST HAVE BEEN

Once again, we were on the "Little Tennessee", the stream upon which our adventure had originally begun, and whose identity had been lost temporarily in the lakes behind us. Now, it was considerably augmented by those same reservoirs, and hurried along over the rocks as if impatient at the time it had lost. The bottom, clearly discernable through the crystalline water, was usually paved with baseball-sized stones, but periodically, it would buckle into shoals of great brown boulders that reached aloft to roll the water's surface with washboard waves.

The "Tippie-Canoe" danced across the slighter ones and pitched and tossed like a young colt over the others. We knew for the first time the exhilaration of real speed and we loved it! The long, placid paddles across the lakes were gone and we were actually whipping past the shore.

After a few miles, the river swung in beside the highway to Maryville, Tennessee, and we could see workmen on the slopes above cutting a new roadbed. This we knew was to accommodate traffic after the completion of Chilhowee Dam, some miles below, which event would impound the river's waters a fourth time and raise the surface level above that of existing traffic facilities.

Suddenly, there was a gigantic roar as if someone had discharged a 12-guage shotgun right in our ears! We both jumped involuntarily and snapped our heads around to see the stream not fifty yards behind us showered with great chunks of granite and debris. A dust cloud rolled out simultaneously to envelope the scene in a Sulphur yellow pall. What a shock! And what a fortunate escape!

The workmen above had flagged down *highway* traffic to blast the new roadbed but had given never a thought to us *river* travelers below the bank. We didn't stay to seek apologies, however, and paddled the next several miles with apprehensive vigor.

Still, we remained mindful that what we were paddling *to* might be even worse than what we were paddling *from*. All along our way, men had warned us about the water diversion around the new Chilhowee project, and we strained our ears for the expected roar of a channel that might claim us before we could reach the shore. Inevitable it came, but not before the half-dozen completed gates, towering in the near distance, announced its presence. We crabbed along the bank to avoid the powerful current and finally drew into to study the situation.

Cofferdams had been sunk across two-thirds of the original riverbed. Behind these rose a massive wall, outlining the great, square overflow sockets. The water swept around the cofferdams to the right, thundered between two sentinel rocks, and finally rocketed off down a long, narrow alley, beneath the low beams of a temporary bridge.

We walked down the bank for perhaps two-hundred yards to survey the turbulence that was thus created. The steepness of the bank kept us from the water's edge, but, from our perch well above it, we could see the battering-ram power that caromed off the two rocks and tore past in a series of great running leaps.

More frightening still was the bridge, whose heavy timbers rested on a close-knit series of tree-like piles. There were only ten to fifteen feet between them, and, as I contemplated the current, I thought to myself what a collision here would do to the boat... and to us. It was going to be like shooting a ball through one of those trick mazes at the miniature golf course.

I walked down to talk with a workman who had come out from the dam side to a tool house half-way across the span. "Anyone ever come through here in a boat?", I queried. "Never saw anyone try it!", he said. "Well, if my wife's willing, you're about to.", I answered. And she was!

First, we pulled off our shoes and tied them to the thwarts. Then, we put on our lifejackets and battened everything else down as well as we could. My heart was in my throat and I knew

Shirley's was too, but we were trying to be brave for each other's sake about that time, and we launched ourselves into the current like children whistling in the dark.

Shirley kneeled flat on the floorboards in the bow with her paddle stowed beside her. I knelt also to keep our weight as low as possible and used my paddle rudder-like to deflect us immediately into midstream. The water's behavior was frantic near the great entrance stones and I knew disaster would be certain if we were drawn too close to either of them.

Fortune smiled and this task was successfully accomplished, but I never dreamed of the fury to come. Suddenly the terrific undercurrent took hold and snatched us forward like a roller-coaster from the peak of its climb. There was no turning back, hardly a chance to breathe. Three and four-foot waves were leaping crazily around us, and Shirley was gathering a lap full of water every time we plunged through one. At once the low bridge was before us and then it was far behind. The canoe had gone squarely between the centermost supports!

We continued to careen wildly along for another quarter of a mile before things quieted down enough to talk about it. Shirley laughed and told me about the construction workers who'd thrown down their tools and run along the bank to see our expected demise. What a show it must have been! My own attention, however, had been riveted on preventing us from swinging around, and it all happened too fast for any appreciation on my part except that wild, free thrill of besting the elements. I felt a little like "Big Mike Fink, the River King".

But we were tired from the excitement, and the sun beamed warmly on our bare arms and legs as the water deepened and slowed beneath us. Gone for a time were the shoals and the blasting; and even the highway had strayed off to leave us in a picturesque world of lovely Tennessee farms and old-fashioned, one-car ferryboats. We lay back against the thwarts and let our canoe cartwheel lazily down the river. This was really "living".

Like all good things, this eventually came to an end, though; We began to realize, after some distance, that the current was playing out too much. There was still many a mile of water between us and our professed goal, and we feared we were running short of time. It seemed such a shame to come so far and yet not do what we'd set out to do, so we took up the paddles and fell into familiar rhythm.

KINDLY TRESPASSING

The generality of our maps continued to plague us. It was difficult to know exactly where we were, or how far we'd come. Our best guideposts were the ferry crossings, though many of them had been discontinued, and only the guide cable strung overhead remained to testify to what once had been.

As day became evening, we began to examine the stream banks for a campsite. They were predominantly in pasture or cultivation, though there were occasional swamps and forests of great length. The mountains had long since fallen behind us, and we were generally in flat, valley country which sometimes wrinkled into low hills and, once, into a sizable Indian burial mound.

About six, we came upon a projecting shoulder of pasture where the river reformed from diverse courses around a long island. There was a sandy beach, on which we landed and unloaded, and a good path up to the grassy pasture floor some six or seven feet higher. A quick survey from this point showed us to be concealed from the owner's farmhouse by a still-higher terrace, and a short reconnaissance located that structure a quarter of a mile away.

Now, why walk all that distance to get camping permission when I'm tired, I reasoned. We'll leave a neat campsite and be gone early in the morning. Those folks will never know we were here. That's the way I figured, but things didn't quite go that way.

About the time I got our tent up and Shirley had supper underway, here came farmer, and son-in-law, grandson, granddaughter, and the dog to fish! Shirley stayed behind while I advanced, clad only in swim-trunks, to negotiate a treaty. I believe my attire in itself so startled the poor man that he listened with unaccustomed meekness to my apologies, and, after a moment's silent consideration, granted technical permission for our de facto presence.

We never became great friends, but, by next morning, when we sought him out again for drinking water, we were great pals with the kids and the dog, knew where his "trot-line" was and with what it was baited, and had what proved to be an extremely inaccurate estimate of how far it was to Lenoir City. Nevertheless, he gave us the water, and he was a prototype in old-fashioned overalls and muddy rubber boots of the individuality this Country's built on.

The next day was much like the former, except that, perhaps, the river current was even more sluggish than before and necessitated constant paddling. There were no longer any shoals of any consequence, so we diverted our minds with the scenes of tractors working the fields and magnificent livestock standing in the high distance beneath Tennessee's ancient cedars. Sometimes, the river would separate into a half-dozen channels winding through an area of swampy islands. At other times, it would narrow between high banks clothes in shrubs and little red flowers. We came to feel at home with it, realizing that, in all the dwellings we passed, probably not one person in a thousand had ever ridden the stream from end to end, as we were doing. Even the great booming take-offs of the gray cranes became commonplace, and we actually enjoyed the exhilaration of outracing the fringes of another storm.

It was then that we became aware how much a part of all the outdoors we'd become. Paddling was no longer a chore, but, rather, a way of life, like walking, and we took it just as much for granted. There was no conscious effort except in the late afternoon, when fatigue began to overtake us. (Later, when we returned home and re-entered our apartment for the first time, we experienced the strangest sensation of oppressiveness that either of us could ever recall.)

THE HOME STRETCH

This was Saturday, a week after Walt had left us at Lost Bridge in North Carolina. It was early afternoon again, and we were less than a dozen miles from the confluence of the "Little Tennessee" and "Tennessee" Rivers at Lenoir City, Tennessee. We stopped at a country crossroads community for groceries and tried to reach our terminal driver, Wally, in Atlanta. But he's an adventurer in his own right and was off camping closer to home. It didn't really matter. We hadn't planned to reach our destination before Monday, and we wanted only to let him know we were in range.

But, the rest of Saturday afternoon carried us unexpectedly down to the river's mouth, and we found ourselves bucking the estuary's high waves just before sundown. To our right and a mile upstream on the "Tennessee" rose the majestic battlements of Fort Loudon Dam, and before us, the spires and rooftops of Lenoir City.

The larger stream, we quickly learned, was a bad place for canoes. Strong winds from the South were kicking up whitecaps and we had either to go directly crosswind or tack downstream against the wind. Since tacking meant dropping below the town's denser settlement, we put on our lifejackets again and rolled through the troughs, straight across. It did us little good, however. There were no docks or business houses in that vicinity, and darkness was nearly on us. There could be no further attempt to call Wally that day, and there would be no camp unless we found a site in a hurry.

That meant a three-mile paddle down-river before we could find another likely-looking pasture and return trip the next morning to seek a telephone again. But still no driver! We knew this meant a wait at the end of the line, for he wouldn't be traveling north as we paddled the last twelve miles south to our rendezvous at Louden, but there was no help for it, and we set out on the last leg of the trip under a murderous sun.

The water beneath us was dirty and rough. We felt awkward and out of place. Occasionally a two-decked steamer would pass, pushing a string of barges, and the surface would roll out from its bows in great tidal waves and then smash back and forth between the stone-ballasted shores like sat-on water in a bathtub. No... it <u>definitely</u> wasn't a place for canoes.

We belonged back in the clear, clean sweeps of Fontana, Cheoah, and Calderwood and the breath-taking race of Chilhowee. So, without reluctance, we rounded one last interminable bend and saw the Louden bridge gleaming silver in the distance.

Wally was a full day reaching the rendezvous, so we had ample time to draw "Tippie-Canoe" up on the bank for a good cleaning and a thorough investigation. The trip's first twelve rugged miles over the river rocks had grated away a little of the keel, and most of the paint was stripped from the bottom, but she was still the stout ship in which we'd started. Today, she's recovered from even these minor wounds and her jutting bow beneath the house seems always to say, "Let's take another canoeing vacation".

A CANOE-CAMPING CHECKLIST
FOR
A CANOEING COUPLE

CANOE AND ACCESSORIES

Canoe (Try a 17-ft. Aluminum!)
Boat Cover
Boat Cushions
Paddles (Carry one spare)
Floorboards
Bailing-can
Large Sponge
Life Jackets
Bow and Stern Lines
Car-top Carrier and Strap-pads
Mooring Chain and Padlock
Carrying Yoke
Waterproof bags (With cardboard box inserts)

NAVIGATIONAL AIDS

Duplicate Navigation and Area Charts
Measuring Dividers
Pencils
Notebook
Compass
Field Glasses

CLOTHING (SUMMER)

Lightweight Trousers
Shorts
Swimsuits
Tee-Shirts

Long-Sleeved Shirts

Lightweight Jackets

Canoe Moccasins or Rubber-Soled Shoes

Long-Billed Caps

Rain Hats or Hoods

Ponchos or Waterproof Parkas

Under-Clothing

Socks

Laundry Bag

MEDICAL AND HYGIENIC SUPPLIES

Liniment

Sunburn Lotion

"Noxema"

Poison Ivy Lotion

Octagon Soap

Hand Lotion

Insect Repellent

Aerosol Bomb

Sunglasses

First-Aid Supplies

Snake Bite Kit

Toilet Kit

Toilet Paper

Shaving Mirror

Sewing Kit and Scissors

Floating Soap and Dish

Bath Towels and Wash Cloths

CAMPING EQUIPMENT AND SUPPLIES

Tent

Kapok Sleeping Bags (or "jungle hammocks")

Air Mattresses

Air Mattress Pump

Extra Blankets (when needed)

Small Tarpaulin

Trenching Shovel and Case

Hand-Axe and Case

Machete and Case

Hunting Knife and Case

Gas Lantern

Electric Lantern

Heavy Cord and Light Rope

Small Can Machine Oil

Whetstone

Canoe Repair Materials

½ doz. Large Corks (for tipping sharp objects)

Pistol or Rifle (and Ammo.)

Alarm Clock and Old Wristwatch

COOKING EQUIPMENT AND SUPPLIES

Gas Stove and Fuel

Reflector Oven

Cooking Kit and Eating Utensils

Large Frying Pan

Aluminum Measuring Cup

Large Fork

Large Spoon

Pancake Turner

Fish Scaler

Potato Peeler

Can and Bottle Opener

Lister Bag (about 2 gal.)

Canteens (2)

Heavy Duty Aluminum Foil

Small Aluminum Pan

Scouring Pads (with soap)

Liquid Detergent

Small Sponges (2)

www.ingramcontent.com/pod-product-compliance
Lightning Source LLC
Chambersburg PA
CBHW020332290526
45785CB00007B/3027